"Written with the humor and confidence Lisa [...] x-hibiting how she has turned a tragedy into an opportunity without it knocking her on her butt! This personal experience has made her more self-reflective and appreciative of living in the moment. Truly inspirational!"

Andrea B. Wilson
FOUNDER AND CHAIRMAN
FOUNDATION FOR SARCOIDOSIS RESEARCH

"Lisa Dietlin reminds us all of how important it is to live our lives to the fullest. Her near tragedy becomes an illumination and investigation of how to change one's life before it's too late."

Andrew Busch
ENGAGED COMMUNICATIONS GROUP

"Lisa's story about a life altering situation should be required reading for everyone that needs to put things in perspective. Every day is a gift and we should not wait until we get hit by a taxi to cherish every millisecond we have with those we love."

Brett Gasper CFP® CPWA®
SENIOR VICE PRESIDENT—WEALTH MANAGEMENT
THE GASPER FINANCIAL GROUP
WEALTH ADVISOR
UBS FINANCIAL SERVICES INC.

"*I Got Hit* hits me where I live with life lessons. *IGHBAT* has tips, turning points and transformation. Lisa is courageous in her transparency and reminds me to share the love we all need to feel."

Dana Wojtan
SEEKER OF TRUTH AND ALL ROUND AWESOME CHICK

"Lisa has spent her entire career helping individuals and institutions reach their highest potential and manifest the truth that lies within each person and organization. Yet it took getting hit by a cab to force her to look inward, to discard some deeply held beliefs about truth, life and success and then manifest and embrace her new normal. Her book is another reminder to us all of what is ultimately most important."

Maryilene Blondell
DIRECTOR OF DEVELOPMENT
THE ALS ASSOCIATION

"Why wait until a tragedy to change your life and realize fulfillment. This uplifting and brief snapshot of time about escaping death by cab is worth a lifetime of wisdom. A roadmap for the challenged to the ultimate destination."

Kim Vatis
FORMER ANCHOR
NBC 5 CHICAGO

"You will enjoy this book! An easy read with sage advice, Lisa takes a life altering potential tragedy and turns it into an important lesson. Lisa, thanks for making a difference!"

Mark Frommer
SENIOR VICE PRESIDENT
MORGAN STANLEY

"I fully agree with your mantras. While I can't always live up to them fully, I have implemented the ideas as part of my daily life—especially my competition prep. Rather than think, 'Can I do this again? Will I win?' I instead choose to focus on using it as a platform to raise awareness for cancer. We all have our close calls in life—whether a vehicle accident, a devastating illness or injury, etc.—it's what we do with it after that matters, I think. Thank you for reminding me of this with your book!"

Heather Sullivan
FIRST PLACE WINNER
MUSCLE BEACH INTERNATIONAL CLASSIC COMPETITION

"Lisa's book was insightful and powerful. She made the ideas accessible, and planted the seeds to make my goals achievable. It was a quick and easy read, and power-packed with the inspiration to get myself motivated!"

Shalini Suryanarayana
UNIVERSITY PROGRAM DIRECTOR AND COMMUNITY SERVICE ACTIVIST

"A simple and poignant story that expresses the deep themes of Victor Frankel's *Mans Search For Meaning* and Elkhart Tolle's *A New Earth: Awaken to Your Life's Purpose*. May we learn our lessons through Lisa's story as to avoid the brick wall or distracted driver. I, for one, am changed."

Elizabeth Martin
EXECUTIVE DIRECTOR
NATIONAL HELLENIC MUSEUM

"In Lisa Dietlin's latest book, she authentically shares with the reader how being hit and then run over by a taxi cab driver was an invaluable wake-up call in helping her to slow down and smell the coffee that is life. Dietlin's beautifully detailed account of the incident and following epiphany, helps us to remember we only get to take this journey once, so do it with grace, happiness and joy in one's heart and, more important, actions. A timely read for those seeking a fuller more meaningful life and lifestyle."

Ralph Amos
VICE PRESIDENT, ALUMNI RELATIONS
USM FOUNDATION, INC.

"Lisa's ability to turn what most would find a tragic, life-glooming incident into an affirming, learning and teaching tool for us all is the epitome of how she looks at and lives her life. Her sharing this story is a reminder to us all to always find happiness and joy...whatever our situation may be."

Kristin Norell
DIRECTOR, INTERNATIONAL SALES
WORLD BOOK

To James and Ryan…

…two men who ran into a street to help a stranger.
I don't know their last names nor what they do or even where they live,
but to me they were real life angels.
What I do know now, because of their selfless acts of generosity,
is that people still do help others in times of need.

Thank you.

Dietlin Entertainment Group
PO BOX 4781 • CHICAGO, IL • 60680 • 773.772.2402

instituteoftransformationalphilanthropy.com

Book Design by Katie LaRosa
ktlarosa.com

Photography of Donald J Pliner shoes by Stephen McMullin

I Got Hit By A Taxi, But You Look Run Over

Life Lessons about Happiness and Joy

Lisa M. Dietlin

Courageous Dreams Publishing House

Chicago, Illinois

ACKNOWLEDGMENTS

This is my sixth book and as usual, there are always so many people to thank. First, appreciation and gratitude is sent to all who showed up in my life and were supportive of me after the accident. The journey and observations of witnessing who shows up in life and who doesn't when tragedy or potential tragedy occurs was an interesting one.

Second, thank you to the first responders who showed up within seconds, then minutes, of the accident. And thanks to James and Ryan, the two strangers who provided help, Rob and Kate, the ambulance team that came from Greektown and the numerous medical personnel who took care of me once I arrived at Northwestern Memorial Hospital.

Third, a big thank you to my family for always being supportive of me. My mom, sister and brother were ready to jump in and be there if needed with each of them offering to come to Chicago from Michigan immediately to provide support and offer assistance. Much love and gratitude goes to Shirley, Linda and Jeff who prove time and time again that they are the anchors in my life. They are always there providing me a safe haven in which to return from time to time.

During this past year, my staff and clients were incredibly understanding and supportive and for that I am truly grateful.

Thank you to all who listened to the story of the accident as it was told. Repeatedly sharing my experience was a cathartic experience. A special thank you to my friends Erin, Aimee, Cathy, Jenniffer (Jen), Therese, Renee, Mary Ann, Barbara, Caroline, Suzanne, Janet, Heather, Kristin, Julia, Jodie, Bernie, Sherry, Valerie, Cibeline, Kurt, Sara, Lisa, Charles, Zeke, Marcy, Anne, Chris, Jan and Charles. All of them quickly reached out and have stayed in touch throughout this process.

Thank you to Grace Foco for editing the early draft of this manuscript. You are truly a gifted young lady who I am blessed to know.

Thank you to Mary Holden for the final editing of this manuscript. Your edits and words of encouragement from the very beginning truly have touched my heart.

And finally, a big thank you to fellow Michigan State University alumni and staff, Sue Petrisin and Lisa Parker (Go Green), for suggesting the title of this book. Those 11 short words have permanently changed my outlook in life; they became the catalyst to sit down and write this book.

TABLE OF CONTENTS

CHAPTER 1
What Life Was Like

Ambitious
Driven
Achiever
Overachiever
Perfectionist
Controlling
Hyper
Energetic

These are the words I often heard used to describe me. However, the one that resonated the loudest and most frequently was:

Hardworking.

"You are such a hard worker, Lisa," is what I was told again and again by friends, colleagues, co-workers, family members and even acquaintances. I distinctly remember the first time I heard that term used to describe me. It was during graduate school, when we had an assignment to create our personal mission statement. As a first step in that process, we were directed to think about people in our lives from different sectors. While thinking of our relationship with that person we were asked to list five to six adjectives they would use to describe ourselves. Once we had the words, we were instructed to have a conversation with these individuals asking them if they agreed. I took on this assignment with my usual hyper, energetic enthusiasm and took care to craft my list of individuals and the words for each relationship. As I suspect the other students did, I chose words such as: kind, generous, helpful, smart, creative, nice, determined, goal-oriented, etc. to describe those connections.

Then I met or talked with everyone on my list and asked them if they agreed with the words I had chosen. During the discussion, each said yes, they agreed with the words I had listed, but all said they wanted to add a word. When I asked what that word would be, every one of them said the same thing: Hardworking.

"Really?"

"Yes!" Every single one of them responded, without hesitation. I was stunned. I was surprised. Until that point in time, I believed I was an average worker and that everyone worked at the same pace I did, or faster. Never once did I think of myself as a hard worker. Not once.

I became irritated and maybe even a little mad wondering sometimes aloud to myself, "Is that what people are going to remember about me? That I am a hard worker? What about all the other things I do or believe I am?"

During this same time, I also happened to participate in a team building exercise at work where we had to list in order our priorities and values from a deck of 50 cards. This meant some value had to be number one and another value had to be number 50. Once again, I jumped in with driven ambition. The top of my list was obvious… courage, authority, integrity. But at the bottom of the list, my least valued priority was fun. This realization stunned me. Maybe my friends were correct; perhaps by saying that I was a hard worker what they were telling me was work was all I did—to the exclusion of everything else.

Even with both of these revelations, I did nothing to change. I received the information but still lived a hardworking and driven life, believing some of those old rules and practices such as:

✓ If it's not hard, it isn't worth it

✓ Things that come too easy and too fast never last

✓ Hard work pays off

I believed stress, frustration, anxiety and worry were integrally tied to the path of success…necessary evils to achieving any level of advancement in one's career and job. In recalling my career, I always worked long hours, weekends and evenings. Frequently, I gave up time with friends, missed special events and rarely found the time to relax. I simply kept going and going often to the point of exhaustion. In fact, three times in my life I have been diagnosed with exhaustion and threatened with hospitalization if I did not make some life changes.

Translation: **RELAX.**

Usually, I would slow down a bit; I might have even taken a day off, but my work and responsibilities were never far from my thoughts. My family dreaded the appearance of my briefcase or laptop as I entered their homes, knowing part of the time spent together would be me hovering over a keyboard or reviewing a report for work. Even with all of these "signs" I never took notice of how the rest of the world behaved in comparison to my style. Everyone saw what I could not see myself. I was an out-of-control, ambitiously driven, hyper energetic **HARD WORKER.**

I recall a story told by correspondent and host of "CBS Sunday Morning," Charles Kuralt, that paralleled the way I lived my life. He shared with viewers that shortly after interviewing a man from Minnesota, he was asked by that man to join him to go fishing in the summer. Every year the invitation would come and every year Charles Kuralt would turn it down while detailing some important work project that just had to be done. Year after year the invitation would be extended and again it would be declined. Then one year, the invitation did not come. Charles assumed the Minnesota man was irritated with him and all the declinations or that he simply decided not to ask anymore. He later learned the man had passed away sometime during the prior year. No more invitations would be forthcoming to go fishing in Minnesota in the summer.

It was then Charles Kuralt realized he could not recall what had been so important in terms of work that he could not go fishing in at least one of those summers. But he did realize if he had gone fishing he would have always remembered that experience.

When I heard this story, I had the sudden realization that this was my life and the choices I often made. After everyone told me who I was and how I lived; then having the realization after hearing this news segment, the real question was: Would I change?

The short answer was, "No."

I did not change. Instead something more profoundly life changing happened.

CHAPTER 2
The Accident

I got hit by a taxi.

As straightforward and simple as that statement appears to describe what happened, it really was a complicated, complex and lasting life change that had occurred.

On Monday, September 8, 2014 at about 8:21 in the evening I was in Chicago's downtown Loop area. I know the time because I had just looked at the numbers either on my iPhone or a clock sign on the street. I was walking from a board meeting to my car in the parking garage near my office, hoping to get 10,000 Fitbit steps in for the day. As always, I was multi-tasking: talking to my mom on the phone, exercising and running in and out of one appointment to the next, which was my usual routine especially at the end of the day.

Then it happened.

I was walking east on Lake Street, crossing Post Street in the crosswalk. As a point of reference, Post Street is a one block street from Lake Street to lower Wacker Drive. Wacker Drive is a multi-level thoroughfare with the upper street intended for local traffic. Lower Wacker Drive is a street that many locals including taxi drivers use to escape the congestion of cars on the above ground streets. It was designed for through traffic and trucks to make deliveries to the various downtown buildings. I've always found it eerily fascinating to drive below the city of Chicago noticing that drivers are required to use headlights while zigzagging the twists and turns of the road in the hopes of finding the right exit to get back to the upper level of Wacker Drive.

As I was walking in the crosswalk, about two-thirds of the way through it, a blue taxi struck me and hit my left leg in the calf which was behind me because I was stepping forward with the right leg. I was propelled on top of the hood of the car landing with incredible force on my butt then my back fell onto the windshield. My head hit the windshield but not hard enough to even cause a spider crack to occur.

As a note to those wondering what this Wacker Drive being described is, I suggest renting the movie "The Blues Brothers" (1980) to watch the scene in which the brothers take the Bluesmobile down the ramp to "the express level." That is lower Wacker Drive. This area was also used in high speed chase scenes for two "Batman" franchise movies including "Batman Begins" (2005) and "The Dark Knight" (2008). In 2015, the television drama, "Chicago PD," used lower Wacker Drive in an episode with a scene about a kidnapped boy on a bus, as do many dramas and shows set in Chicago.

At this point I was thinking two things: Why does my bottom jaw hurt so much? And, where am I? It was then I realized I was sliding clockwise on the hood of the taxi due to the driver braking, turning 180 degrees until I was facing the windshield with my feet pointed toward the taxi driver. I could see him. His face was filled with terror.

During that turning process, everything felt like it was moving in slow motion. The buildings, signs and even the "L" (the elevated train) going by at a pace so measured and unhurried that I had time to have two more distinct thoughts. I wondered if I was moving at such a slow pace, how long could it last? Then I asked myself, "How am I going to get off the hood of this car?"

Next I had the very strange realization that I still had my purse on my right shoulder and my briefcase bag on my left one. And that I was still moving. I was sliding backwards off the car and was going to hit the ground. I flew off the taxi and landed a few feet in front of it, once again on my butt, with my knees bent. I felt my head flying backwards, about to hit the asphalt pavement of the street, so I immediately threw my arms and hands down toward the road to prevent the back of my head from hitting the ground.

Now I was a few feet in front of the taxi but the vehicle was not stopping. It was still moving and coming directly towards me. I was panicked; I knew there was not enough time to get out of the way. As I was coming face to face with the right front tire, I was sure this was the end.

I was convinced I was going to die right there, right then, by being run over by a taxi. I remember thinking, "I survived being hit by the taxi, I survived landing on the taxi and I survived falling off the hood of the taxi. Now I am going to be run over by the taxi and at 51 years of age, I am going to die."

But, I lived—miraculously and incredibly, I lived. The taxi did drive over about two thirds of my body before stopping at my upper ribs. I was under the taxi, but still breathing. Still alive. Still trying to process what had just happened.

Then everything stopped. And for an instant I was simply happy to be…to be breathing, to be alive, to be in no pain. Then things started moving again.

First, the car needed to be moved off my body. The taxi driver had put the car in reverse and started moving backwards up Post Street without ever checking on me first. Truth be told, it was at this point in time that I was most scared because it appeared to me the driver was not only moving the car off my body but might actually be leaving; leaving me alone in the middle of what I imagined was a deserted, dark street. I remember thinking, "Don't leave…please don't leave me alone in this street."

At this moment, I saw two men running towards me. They had heard and seen what had happened and were running to help me. The driver of the taxi had finally stopped his car, got out and was running toward me, too.

I started crying. Help was coming. There were people running towards me. I was alive.

The two men, who I later found out were named James and Ryan, knelt down beside me and asked if I was all right. I was dazed and couldn't focus. I told them I needed to find my phone to call my mom and tell her I was OK because I had been talking to her when I got hit.

They knew I was in shock and tried to calm me down by agreeing with this request as ridiculous as it might seem. But first they wanted to lay me down flat on my back as I was still resting on my arms with my purse and briefcase hanging off my shoulders. I said no. I knew everything was working in the position I was in and terrified to be touched and/or moved.

The taxi driver kept saying he was sorry; that he didn't mean to hit me. I responded by acknowledging what he was saying but realizing at this point, comforting him was not my primary concern, nor did it appear to be a concern to James or Ryan. The two of them made a plan—one was going to call 911 and the other was going to direct the traffic that was traveling on this street. The one calling 911 was also going to stay with me.

During this period of time while I was lying on the ground, I was encouraged by a number of people who stopped their cars or stopped during their walk to offer assistance and help. Strangers really do help strangers.

The ambulance was called. We called my mom to tell her about the accident and then we called my "ICE" (In Case of Emergency) person.

At this point of the ordeal, the taxi driver suggested I get up and walk around. Both James and Ryan told me not to do it. Later, I learned that if you are able to walk after being hit by a car, it is assumed that you are OK and it is more difficult to file an insurance claim or sue for damages.

The four of us continued to wait. I was still crying, still on the ground, leaning back on my arms waiting for the ambulance to arrive. It must have seemed like we were waiting a long time, especially

to the taxi driver, who suggested that James and Ryan put me in the back of his car so he could drive me to the hospital. Again, the two men denied his request. I was not going to be put in the back of his car or any car. They stated that we'd continue to wait for the ambulance. I was relieved to know someone was looking out for me, taking charge and most of all, making good decisions.

The sound of sirens could be heard in the distance. The fire engine Advanced Life Support (ALS) and ambulance arrived; they'd come from the Greek-town firehouse station. Two EMS workers, Rob and Kate, hopped out of the ambulance to help me.

Throughout the accident, I kept asking people their names in order to remain conscious and sense what was happening. Kate tended to me, asking my name and checking my vitals. Rob asked if I had taken off my shoes.

I looked down and saw I had no shoes on my feet—only my socks. I cried hard. I told Rob that no, I had not taken my shoes off and asked, "Where are my shoes?"

The shoes were made by designer Donald J. Pliner. They have a high ankle opening so I often have to use a shoehorn to get them on my feet.

I saw the exchange of looks between Rob and Kate and knew this accident had just been elevated from bad to really bad.

Rob, James and Ryan looked for my shoes and eventually found one on the east side of the street lying next to the curb and sidewalk; the other shoe was on the west side of the street on the sidewalk.

This was when I realized I'd been hit hard enough to blow my shoes off.

Once the shoes were found, Kate announced that I was going to the trauma emergency room at Northwestern Memorial Hospital and she placed a call informing the dispatcher of the destination. They put a neck collar on to stabilize me. They slid a board under my body and strapped me on it. One of the men who rushed in to help me had to leave to go back to work; I thanked him as he left. The other stayed with the EMS team until I was loaded into the ambulance.

I don't remember a lot about the ride to the hospital except the loud sirens and our arrival. Upon entering the hospital and being rolled into a room, I do remember a doctor introducing himself and telling me that a lot of people were going to be working on me. I was pricked with needles, attached to monitors and then I realized what trauma ER really meant.

It meant the medical professionals were going to cut off all my clothes. Immediately I thought what most likely every woman in the same situation would think: "Do my bra and underwear match?" Then I thought, "Dang, my mom was right…always wear clean underwear."

The trauma team went to work on me. In addition to the standard picking, poking and prodding, they did every test that seemed standard (and not standard) to the victim of a hit and run-over, including a CT-scan, x-ray, blood draw, etc. The results kept coming back negative! They showed I had no internal or external damage, including a lack of cuts and bruises.

During the times between tests, the gurney on which I was laying was placed into the hallway and under a sign with the words "Decontamination Shower." At the time I wondered if this was a message for me. I later came to realize it was indeed a personal message to me. My life was about to take a huge turn—180 degrees—again.

An emergency room on any night is busy with both patients and medical personnel coming and going. In the background is always the wail of the siren with ambulances and other first responder vehicles arriving and departing.

This is when it happened. The message that I had long been ignoring in my life was first heard.

While laying on the gurney among all the commotion and noise, waiting to be taken for another test, I heard a voice. It was a distinct voice that was loud and clear. This voice was speaking directly to me. Here is what I heard...

"It's all bullshit except happiness and joy."

Now people who know me realize I rarely use curse words and even more rarely use the word "bullshit." It's just not my go-to swear word. With that being said, I was sure it wasn't me saying something like this in my head. So I began, as much as I could from a gurney point of view, to look around for the person who was making this statement because it kept repeating, "It's all bullshit except happiness and joy."

As I observed the emergency room, I saw other patients on gurneys with family and friends standing or sitting next to them. Some were talking, but in hushed voices. I noticed medical personnel walking in and out of exam rooms or behind curtains but did not see anyone talking loud enough for me to hear. But it was still there. Over and over. "It's all bullshit except happiness and joy."

I wasn't scared of the voice.

I didn't ask anyone else if they heard it.

I knew it was a message from the Universe; meaning from God, to me.

Direct.

Simple.

And in a type of statement I would comprehend and remember.

A sense of calm came over me.

A peace let me feel that everything was going to be OK.

Instead of wondering who was making this statement, I had a knowing realization it was true. I accepted it as pure fact. It was as if I had known this truth for my entire life. It was at this moment of realization I noticed a change in me that continues to this day.

As I lay on that gurney in a hospital emergency room in downtown Chicago having been struck, tossed around and run over by a taxi cab, I realized the accident really wasn't the important event in my life on which I needed to focus.

I needed to focus on the happiness and joy within me.

Some people might question that assertion by asking if I really was happy and joyful about the fact that I got hit and run over by a taxi. My response is an emphatic yes.

Because I got hit and run over by a taxi, I knew the happiness and joy of being alive.

I knew the happiness and joy of being able to breathe.

I knew the happiness and joy of being able to remember my name and who I was…in essence I was remembering me.

I knew the happiness and joy of not being physically hurt.

I knew the happiness and joy of being able to think.

And I knew the happiness and joy of a life's transformation happening in an instant.

The Chicago police officer at the scene of the accident arrived at the hospital brought me back to reality. She was there to give me the accident report. As I lay there under the "Decontamination Shower" sign with the voice in my head still repeating, "It's all bullshit except happiness and joy," the policewoman shared with me that the driver had been ticketed. She told me that the court date was October 5. And, if I did not show up in court on that date, the ticket would be automatically dismissed. As she left, she mentioned being relieved that I was OK.

But I was incredulous about the process she'd just described! I decided to deal with it later.

Diagnostic tests continued. More results were received. All indicated I was fine. There was no damage.

Still in disbelief and wonderment from the results of my tests, I overheard one doctor ask the other the following, "Has she been drinking?"

The other doctor said, "No, there are no drugs or alcohol in her system."

At that point, I piped up from the gurney and shared that I had been headed home to have a glass of wine. Everyone laughed.

The most frightening part of being in the hospital was getting everything to move again. Let me explain. After the exhaustive testing proved there was no internal damage and the exam by both the EMS workers and the medical team showed no external damage, it was time to get me ready to leave the hospital. But first the doctors needed to see if I could move—starting with my feet. One of the doctors stood at the foot of my gurney and folded back the sheet so my feet were sticking out.

He said, "Lisa, we are going to see if you can move your feet." He then asked, "Lisa, can you move your feet?"

I responded, "Yes, just give me a minute."

It must have been a long time because the next thing I remember is the doctor saying again, "Lisa, can you move your feet?"

I replied, "Yeah I think so but I just can't remember how that works." Panic arose as did thoughts of paralysis and the impact it would have on my life. But the doctor was calm.

I remember his soothing voice saying, "That's OK. Let's take it one foot at a time."

He then moved to the end of my right leg near my foot and said, "Let's focus on your right foot. Can you imagine pushing on a gas pedal?" and as he said this he moved his hand up and down like a foot on a gas pedal in a car.

I replied, "Oh yes, I can do that." My right foot began moving.

He then did the same thing with my left foot, and while my calf was really hurting, it did move some.

The doctor then repeated the same questioning about me moving and lifting my head off the gurney. I said I could do that and then was not able to recall how to actually move my head. The doctor's voice was soothing. His simple hand gestures again helped me to lift and move my head.

Later, I was asked what I thought had happened that caused me to temporarily not be able to move. I believe that my chakras were out of alignment. The energy, or spirit, of my body was not in alignment with my physical being. It was as if I had to literally settle back into my body in order for it to move.

At 12:45 a.m., after approximately four and half hours of testing, a nurse announced that if I could walk and drink some ginger ale I could leave the hospital. I did both and was ready to go home. It was then I realized the only available clothing I had were the paper scrubs they had given me. And, I was in need of some footwear. So, I had to put back on the shoes that had been blown off my feet earlier in the evening. For those wondering, the clothes I had been wearing which had been cut off of my body were now in an oversized, clear, plastic bag and simply handed to me.

As I was escorted out of the hospital in a wheelchair, the nurse pushed the call button to signal that I needed transportation. I was not allowed to drive myself home. The bizarre irony was that I had to enter a taxi cab to make my way home! But I wasn't afraid because that voice and message about happiness and joy was still running through my head.

When I arrived home I asked the driver if he could watch me to make sure I made it into the house. I told him I'd been hit and run over by a taxi earlier in the evening. He seemed stunned but agreed to watch me as I made my way into my home. To my surprise, I slept very well that night.

During the next few days, at any moment, I could still feel the sensation of being on the hood of the car. It was as if in a second I could believe I was still there—stuck in the slow motion of time—but knew I was not. It seemed to me that the extent of the damage and change was some psychological or emotional trauma.

Or so I thought....

CHAPTER 3

Statistics about Pedestrians and Cars

Every two hours a pedestrian is killed in a traffic crash.

That means 12 people a day; 84 people a week; 360 people a month; 4,380 people each year die by simply being in a crosswalk or walking when they are hit by an automobile. According to a study sponsored by AARP and Smart Growth America, between 2003 and 2012, a total of 47,000 pedestrians were killed, and 676,000 were injured, throughout the United States. These numbers are astonishing.

After the accident I thought about the people I knew who had been involved in pedestrian/vehicle accidents. The first to come to mind was my good friend Jan from Dallas who while in Chicago on business was hit in a crosswalk. She believes she was hit by one car and run over by another, which caused her leg to break.

I remembered that my oldest nephew who is now a young adult was hit by a car while he was riding a bicycle in a crosswalk. He was about three or four years old when an older man driving a station wagon turned into him. My nephew was knocked off his bike and a chunk of his bike helmet was missing. The driver's mirror was also damaged and hanging off of its base. In the end, my nephew was shaken up, but all right.

Then there is the story of when my mom arrived at my brother's house one weekend to inform us she had hit a bicyclist...or rather the bicyclist had hit her vehicle. He'd darted out of an alley as he pedaled to the local high school football game. The bicycle hit the car on the front right panel and the young man was propelled onto the hood of the vehicle causing the windshield to spider-crack. He, too, walked away unhurt although he did spend time in the hospital that night.

About two months after my accident, a friend of mine joined me for lunch. As she sat down at the table she was bemoaning the fact she'd just learned she had gained ten pounds. She thought her overeating was related to stress. She then told me that she and her mother had been hit by a car in a crosswalk on October 17th. Her mom landed on the hood of the car and she, while being hit by the car, was pushed out of the way. They both were transported to the local hospital. While in the emergency room, she learned from the staff that they had been seeing a pronounced increase in pedestrian and vehicle accidents, which they attributed in part due to distracted driving.

Based on my personal experience and knowledge, the numbers from the study of pedestrians hit, injured and killed by vehicles seemed accurate. But then I wondered why some people survive accidents with vehicles weighing on average 4,000 pounds while others die or are severely injured. My own research led me to conclude that the speed of the vehicle hitting the pedestrian whether walking or on a bicycle was what determined if someone was likely to survive being hit.

In 2012, there was a bill in the New York state senate which provided some statistics regarding how reducing speed limits could reduce pedestrian fatalities. Listed in the *West Side Rag* (www.westsiderag. com/2014/05/02/city-to-reduce-broadway-speed-limit-to-25-mph), the bill stated, "[I]f a pedestrian is hit at 40 mph there is about a 7 in 10 chance of being killed. At 35 mph, there is a 5 in 10 chance of being killed. At 30 mph, there is a 1 in 5 chance of being killed. If the speed limit were lowered to 25 mph, the chance of an accident resulting in death drops significantly to 1 in 10. Another benefit to having a speed limit of 25 mph is the marked improvement in vehicle stopping distance. At 25 mph, stopping distance is improved by 45 feet (23%), which will allow many crashes to be avoided altogether."

This means that 90 percent of the people hit by cars traveling 20 miles per hour survive while only 35 percent survive when hit by a car going 45 miles per hour. Many states are passing laws reducing speeds within cities from 30 mph to 25 mph in the hopes of increasing the survival rates of pedestrians being hit by vehicles.

I wanted to know what could cause a motorist to hit a pedestrian in a crosswalk. In discussing this question with various people, we decided that it must be distracted driving. Not just texting—consider the ever complex, complicated and sophisticated vehicles on the roads now that offer everything from a digital readout of your travel time with turn by turn instructions on GPS, to back up or side view cameras that signal when objects are too close for comfort to the name of your favorite song on the radio including the artists and when the song was released. If you add the use of cell phones into the equation with drivers being distracted by calls ringing, texts pinging, ear phones plugging in or falling out, Bluetooth technology, cigarette lighter battery charging and difficult or emotion-charged conversations, it seems like a perfect storm gathering to target pedestrians.

But there are other contributing factors. Pedestrians who do not cross in designated areas is one reason often cited. One thing that can be done with an eye toward pedestrian safety on streets and roads is lengthening the time for traffic signals which many say are too short. Also, creating boulevards with raised medians allow pedestrians to pause when crossing. Most suburbs were designed for moving vehicles, not for pedestrian safety. The law about turning right on red should be repealed as accidents happen because drivers are often focused on beating the traffic; they're looking left at the road traffic but not right at the pedestrian traffic.

Another startling fact is the segment of our society that has the highest incidence of being hit and dying because of pedestrian/vehicle accident. The answer is senior citizens; those 65 years and older have the highest percentage of pedestrian deaths. The pedestrian/vehicle accidents involving seniors comprise 21 percent while they are only 13 percent of the population. According to the National Complete Streets Coalition's list citing "The 10 Most Dangerous Cities for Pedestrians" for the years between from 2003 to 2012 they were:

1. Orlando, Florida
2. Tampa, Florida
3. Jacksonville, Florida
4. Miami, Florida
5. Memphis, Tennessee
6. Birmingham, Alabama
7. Houston, Texas
8. Atlanta, Georgia
9. Phoenix, Arizona
10. Charlotte, North Carolina

While all of these are southern locations within the United States, the accidents and near misses I have learned of, both before and after my accident, have taken place in the Midwest, primarily Illinois and Michigan and occurred to people under the age of 65. This information made me pause to wonder if the demographics would be changing with the advent of smart cars, hands-free calling and the increase of cars that allow for distracted driving. Perhaps a study done post-2012 will show different results. My guess is that the numbers will increase; the average age will increase as people live longer, but still disproportionately affect people who are senior citizens.

Weekly, if not daily, I now read and hear news reports as well as stories about individuals being hit by moving vehicles. Most of them end by reporting severe injuries or death. Why I escaped unharmed is the question that haunts me. Was it to learn the lesson of the importance of happiness and joy in life?

CHAPTER 4
The Response

The next day after my accident, September 9, was a Tuesday.

As a point of reference, I tell people that Tuesday is my favorite day of the week. Why Tuesday? First, I was born on a Tuesday so in a way I want to honor that day by liking it best. Second, I believe Tuesday is the most overlooked day of the week so I elevate its status by liking it. I mean, no one says, "Thank goodness it's Tuesday!" It's a unique and different weekday, which is what I like about it.

But on this Tuesday, the day after being literally swept off my feet, I was mentally determined to make this day like every Tuesday before the accident. I didn't want it to be unique or different in any way. I just wanted everything to be like it was before the accident.

So, after arriving home and getting into bed by about 1:30 in the morning, I woke up around 6:30 to get ready for work. The thought of staying home to rest after such trauma, and not going into work, simply did not occur to me as I had meetings to attend and a phone call with a major client in the afternoon. That morning I got ready with relative ease, noticing only a few aches and pains primarily radiating from my left leg calf area. Soon, I was locking my front door and beginning the four-block walk to catch the "L" for a commute to downtown Chicago and my office.

I arrived at the usual time, around 8:20, and again found myself the first one in the office. This was not unusual as I was often the first member of the team to arrive at work. Looking back now, it seems strange but at the time I really wanted things to appear and be normal again.

My staff began arriving at the office around 8:30. About 9, I asked them to meet with me at 9:15. I told them I needed to share something with them. When everyone gathered in my office, I said, "I was hit and run over by a taxi last night."

Silence. Then questions: "What?" and "What are you talking about?" and "Why are you here?"

I responded by assuring them I was all right and this was where I wanted to be but felt they needed to know in case something happened during the day. Everyone returned to work, but for me, work and life had already changed.

My first realization of this change occurred during an impromptu phone call from a coordinator of a program in which I was scheduled to be a participant. During the discussion with Julie, my mind wandered back to the accident and the feeling of being hit (as well as the sensation of riding on the hood of the taxi) kept coming back to me. At one point when I was providing a response to a question Julie had asked, I thought to myself, "...am I even making sense? Is what I'm saying an appropriate response? Should I tell her what happened in case I am not making sense? If I tell her will she withdraw the offer for me to participate?"

Again, work and getting things done superseded everything else.

Later in the morning, my friend Therese Rowley, Ph.D. arrived in the office as she shares space on the floor where my company is located. She seemed to know that something was different and asked if I was all right. I told her the story...and then I asked Therese a question... something that had been nagging me for the past few hours since hearing the voice in the hospital.

I asked her if she thought it was strange that since the accident I wanted to send a love letter to all those people I love and who are or were important to me. I went on, saying it occurred to me that only at the time of death or grave illness do we find the courage to tell others how we feel and what someone's role or personality had meant to us. I wanted to tell people now– today–that they were important to me. Therese encouraged me to do it.

When I got home that evening, I began writing my *love letter* email message to be sent to all the people who mean a great deal in my life. It took me quite a while to draft this message that I sent via email later that night…and throughout the next three days. I wanted the recipients to know what had happened but I to also wanted them to know I was OK and just possibly better than OK. Each message was personalized and sent either to individuals or to a group of people who were aligned with me in some capacity. I concluded this email with lines similar to these:

> So with all that said…I want to share that I am really glad you are in my life! I am blessed to call you my friend! And most of all, I am glad to still be here to spend more time with you. Here's to living life fully, making time for fun and creating more amazing memories. Happiness and Joy.

Once each love letter email was in a final draft, I hit the send button—not knowing what to expect. It was about 9:30 on Tuesday evening. I wondered, "What would the response be from those to whom I sent the message?"

The first email response came seven minutes later from my dear friend Leticia:

> YOU made me cry first because YOU are my friend and you where [sic] hurt AND then because I am so appreciative of YOU and your words! LOVE YOU SISTER/AMIGA

The second response, 48 minutes later, was from my good friend Valerie who lives in New Mexico:

> Wow. Yikes. And weird too! Oh my gosh I'm so glad you are here to tell the story the next day. That could have ended very differently. Are you sure you are ok emotionally? You might have some after effects later and need to talk to someone. You might be more sore tomorrow. Take the day off! Hope the Donald Pliners are ok!

As you might guess by her comment, Valerie and I share a love of shoes!

The third response came about two hours later from my high school best friend Annette who lives in the metro Detroit area:

> Oh my God...I'm so happy you are OK. It sounds like a miracle and your guardian angel was by your side. You are one tough woman but please let me know if you need anything. Love you my friend!!!

My college best friend, Caroline, who lives in New York sent a response the next morning:

> Lisa, I'll have to read this a few more times to 'fully digest.' Glad you're ok. Does this mean you won't be posting from the gym this morning? Love, Caroline

Then my kindergarten and lifelong Best Friend Forever (BFF) Cathy sent the following message from our shared hometown of Montrose, Michigan,

"OMG, I'm so glad you're ok. Life truly can change in the blink of an eye. Something to always remember and not take one minute for granted. I love you my BFF and so glad you are still here with me!! Hope your calf feels better soon. Watch out for those crazy taxi drivers, apparently they are not watching out for you :(Have a great day!! XOXOXO

Before I left for work Wednesday morning, I received a phone call from my longtime friend Erin. She was crying. She said she could hardly fathom the words from the email. Erin was about to move to Chicago to take a new position and it would be the first time in 16 years we would be living the same city. During the phone call it seemed we both realized how easily our friendship could have ended because of a freak accident.

While talking to Erin that morning, many other friends were calling. Most left voicemail messages that were some of the most amazing heartfelt comments I have ever received in my life.

It seemed the words I had written, which were honest and transparent, had struck a chord with those who received it. Some of the words and messages brought tears to my eyes while others validated my view of the friendship I had with that person.

One of the very special calls came on Wednesday night from my good friend, Jenniffer Weigel. Jen worked for the *Chicago Tribune* and is a reporter, actor, author and all around great person who is always smiling and has a keen sense or awareness of the fragility of life. During our phone discussion (after we had talked about my accident and Jen was confident I was all right) she shared with me how tough the past few days had been due to her college friend's wife being struck by a falling tree while riding a bicycle with him in one of the Cook County Forest Preserves. Her name was Molly Glynn and she was an actress. She'd had a recurring role as a doctor on the NBC drama series "Chicago Fire."

Jen wondered aloud about the two accidents as if asking herself why one of us (Molly) did not survive an unbelievable freak situation that most would think could never occur and the other (meaning me) did survive a seemingly impossible situation of being hit by a taxi going 35 mph.

Silence ensued as we both pondered the statement and question she had posed.

Then I said, "You know…by all accounts, if you told those two stories to anyone asking them to guess who would survive and who would die, everyone would say I should be the one who is dead, not Molly."

Then I told Jen about the voice I heard in the hospital that told me life is all about happiness and joy. We moved into one of our 'woo-woo' talks—as I like to call them—the talk that close friends have about coincidences, synchronicities and the ultimate complexity of life.

Upon ending the call we said I love you to each other and Jen announced she was going to write a blog about what had happened with her reactions as well as observations. Being an author and columnist, it's how she communicates best and processes her feelings.

A few weeks later, her blog was posted on her website. Jen has given me permission to share this reprint in my book.

Good vs. bad
September 24, 2014

In case you've been living under a rock, a tragic thing happened to actress Molly Glynn a couple of weeks ago. She and her husband Joe Foust were riding bikes in a forest preserve when a storm came through, knocking down a tree that killed Molly.

I found out after the accident that Molly used to have a fear of riding bikes, having gotten hit by a car when she was younger, so Joe promised to only take Molly on paths where cars weren't allowed. Joe and Molly rode bikes more than most, loving every minute of it.

So the person who conquered her fears of riding a bike gets killed by a tree while riding her bike.

What's the deal, God??

I went to college with Joe, and while I only met Molly a few times, she was genuine and loving. When her organs were donated to give life to others, Joe said "Her heart was so big, I'm surprised it fit in anyone else's body."

A few days after Molly's death, I was told of another terrible accident— my friend Lisa got hit by a cab in the Loop that was going 35 miles an hour. She was knocked clear out of her shoes, landing flat on her back in the road. One would think after such a blow, that she too would have died. While emotionally, Lisa's a bit rattled, she escaped the accident with only a few bruises.

So why does one story end in tragedy, while the other seems miraculous?

I've interviewed a lot of spiritual folks who claim to have answers to some of life's biggest head-scratchers. I had to go back into my "woo-woo" rolodex to gain some wisdom after these two back-to-back incidents. The story that seemed to help the most was this blog post that I wrote a couple of years ago when I found out my college friend Marla was killed by a truck after dropping her daughters off at school.

Why do bad things happen to good people?

In that blog post, I wrote about a woman I interviewed named Dr. Mary Neal who not only died in a kayaking accident and came back to life to talk about it, but she also had to bury her son when he was just 19. Since then she's been on "The Today Show", CNN, and every network you can think of talking about her brush with death and her book To Heaven and Back.

"I'm a pragmatist!" She told me. "I couldn't make this stuff up if someone put a gun to my head."

And then she said something I will never forget: "I can't tell you how many times over the last 13 years where something terrible has happened where someone says 'Isn't that terrible about that boating accident?' and I think 'No actually, it was a great gift.'"

"A tragedy is a great gift?" I asked.

"If you think about 'bad' things—think about Jesus—he was betrayed, he was arrested, he was beaten, humiliated, and he was killed. That's bad. By all accounts we should look at that and say 'That's the most horrible thing you can imagine.' But look what came of it. For more than 2000 years people are remembering his story and using it to heal and love. So can you look at that and say it was horrible, but I look at the affect it had on the last 2000 years and it's incredible. He brought a covenant of love. You can look at every bad thing that happened and almost always there are incredibly good things that come of it. You know change doesn't happen when things are easy. Change happens when things aren't easy and when you are pushed. So I would say there is no such thing as good and bad. It just is. And we may not understand it."

I'm not sure I can get to the place where I'm thinking, "There's no such thing as good and bad." I see bad things happening every day through the text alerts from this job—death, fires, accidents where a friend's wife gets killed by a tree. All these things seem pretty bad from my lens.

But I'm trying to do the best I can to embrace Dr. Mary Neal's philosophy—because even with all that is bad, we have miracles too. My friend Lisa escaping with only a bruise after being plowed down by a cab is indeed a miracle.

One thing I do know is this—these incidents were wake-up calls. Life is too short to spend any time with people who don't appreciate you or treat you with respect. Get rid of those people you loathe and hold onto those that you love, because you never know when that person you just talked to will no longer be there to answer the phone.

And as Joe said on his Facebook feed, "Be kind. Love hard. Remember."

Jenniffer Weigel

My response to reading this blog was and still is…wow. Every single time I read it, I am moved by Jen's restatement of Joe's words. "Be Kind. Love Hard. Remember."

Those words made me wonder: Was I saved for a reason?

The responses to my email love letter continued to arrive. This one was from my longtime friend Janet, who lives in D.C.:

> Holy crap! That is amazing. I bet everything slowed down and you were hyper aware of your thoughts and what a ridiculous way to go that would be. I'm so glad you're relatively unscathed. Did they keep you overnight at the hospital? Was the cab driver arrested, impaired, fined? Maybe your next career could be as a stuntwoman. I'm so grateful you're in my life too. You are one tough woman.

My friend Valerie put an exponent on her emailed response by sending a letter postmarked four days after the accident, on September 12th:

> Dear Lisa,
> I'm weeks behind in reading *The NY Times Magazine*. I read this article right after we spoke on the phone tonight. I wonder if a dozen people already sent it to you! It has some similarities with your story. I'm so grateful this crazy experience for you ended the way it did. Whew! ....
>
> Until then...XO
> Valerie

The article she sent was from the August 10, 2014 issue of *The New York Times Magazine* titled "The Driver: His carelessness left me feeling angry and alone. But I didn't really know him."

In this article, the writer, René Steinke, who was struck by a bus, escaped as I did without a scratch (although she had a mild concussion and terrible headache). She, like me, did wonder about the driver of the bus and his carelessness. And as she writes in the article, "Ten days or so after the incident, I received a get-well card in the mail. The card was covered in sparkles, and featured a ribbon bouquet of roses. Inside, a message was written in pencil: 'You have no idea how lucky you are to be alive. God has given you a gift. Every day.'" It was from the driver causing René to realize that he was most likely plagued by terrors and guilt about the bus he was driving when it hit her body.

Although I didn't know it, this article was a sign of what was coming next for me...and the cab driver who'd intersected my body and my life. I set it aside and continued to focus on the responses that kept appearing in emails.

Another friend from high school wrote this, and gave me the idea for this book:

> Lisa,
>
> That is crazy and so glad to hear that you came through the ordeal physically unscathed. Were the shoes ok as well? Just kidding (trying to bring a bit of levity to the situation). Hopefully after a week or so the mental impact of the ordeal will not be so fresh.
>
> I think you need to capture your thoughts on what happened now, in as much detail as possible, as this may just be the meat for a book that you were looking for. You know, "lemons into lemonade."
>
> Keep us posted on how you are doing...
> G.R.

A few days later, I received this email from a former classmate urging me to write this story.

> My dearest Lisa:
>
> I can't even believe that your story below is real........ Actually seems surreal!
>
> This absolutely should be the basis of your next book since your recollection of the play by play is so colorful.......as if you

actually lived it.

With all kidding aside, I am very happy to hear that you are fine and healing quickly. It obviously wasn't your time to leave us on this earth, unlike your local Chicago actress that was suddenly struck by the tree in the last storm while riding her bike.

I too am glad that you are still in my life and blessed to have you as my friend since our high school days. Thank God you are still alive and I wish you a speedy, full recovery.

Have fun, live joyful and continue to create lasting memories!!!

Christopher

My good friend, Father Zeke, sent an email providing great detail of what he would have done for my funeral if the worst had happened and it even included a mariachi band! Everyone responded in such kind ways with amazing words and sentiments.

Bertice (Bertie) Berry, Ph.D. called a few days after I sent the email. During the soliloquy of my litany of reasons of why I was able to walk away without any significant damage, she stopped me and said, "You were saved because all the good you have put out there came back to save you." She went on to say I'd experienced the law of attraction; I'd gotten from life what I'd given to life.

"Could that be true?" I thought to myself. Was living a life of giving back and doing good for others the reason I walked away in one piece from being hit by a taxi traveling 35 mph? Or, was the "attraction," the "match," in that I "hit so hard" my stride, my life—by working so much—that I had to be "hit so hard" in the literal sense in order to wake up, slow down and enjoy the fruits of my labors?

About three weeks after my accident, my friend Andrea would be in town for a visit—she lives in California. But she also said that she wasn't feeling so well, so our time to catch up would be limited. Andrea is the founder of the Foundation for Sarcoidosis Research (FSR), a nonprofit. She has sarcoidosis, often referred to as sarcoid, a disease involving the inflammation of organs.

Andrea also has a positive and sunny disposition on life and all things. It should be noted we have had many, many good belly laughs together to the point of almost forgetting about what we found so amusing.

On the day we met, Andrea was still not feeling well and I was still recovering so we decided to take a long walk on the shores of Lake Michigan. When we parted later in the afternoon, each of us realized again that our friendship was of the utmost importance in our lives even though we now live more than 2,000 miles from each other.

Later that day, she sent the following text to me:

> Lis—it was so so great to see you today!! I must admit that I am in a bit of shock hearing about your accident and about your last year, I don't know why. There seem to be so many facets of the accident and of how you continue on– landing on your feet or butt, not being able to move then slowing down a bit, being grounded...The list goes on and on as does the symbolism. I just can't stop thinking about it! It's so rich with meaning that it's fascinating to dissect!! It's as though you have been given a whole new life!! I'm so excited for you!! Please take it slow and don't do too much, though. As always I'm here to chat whenever!! Thanks for making the time to get together!!! I loved it! Be well, My dear! Xoxo, Andrea

For several weeks and even months after the accident, when someone outside of my inner circle of friends would learn of the accident, they insisted on treating me to a meal, drink or cup of coffee. This still happens on occasion, and it always makes me smile to realize how easy it is to be kind when someone has been involved in or with a difficult situation.

Like the experience of that mysterious voice I heard telling me it's all bullshit except happiness and joy, Joe's words are also worth repeating: "Be Kind. Love Hard. Remember."

CHAPTER 5

What Happened to the Driver?

To this day, that is the question I'm asked most often. But I'm asked other questions, too:

1. Are you still all right?
2. Did they catch the guy?
3. You sued the guy, right?

The answers are yes, yes and no.

Yes, I am still all right. The post-traumatic stress symptoms lingered for awhile, but are mostly gone by now, although there have been subtle changes in my life. The first thing I noticed was my desire for milk. I hadn't drank milk in years but now was choosing it as my beverage for my meals. The second thing I noticed is that when something stressful happens, I spend little time thinking about the negative aspects and begin contemplating the happiness and joy part of the situation. Some days I am a little more emotional than others. And sometimes still when I close my eyes, I can still feel the sensation of being on the hood of the taxi. But that is the extent of the post-traumatic stress symptoms.

Yes, they caught the driver! He had to put the vehicle in reverse to back it off my body. And as shared earlier, he did stop the vehicle.

No, I didn't sue.

These answers, especially the last one, always seem to surprise people. It never occurred to me to bring litigation against the driver—until people started asking me the question. I learned I didn't have much of a case, as my medical prognosis was good. I knew I had to appear in court, however, and that was a problem.

The court appearance date conflicted with a client event I was scheduled to attend in another state. My assistant called the number provided on the accident report several times to ask if the court date could be changed. Every time she called she got "no" for an answer. The date could not be changed and again she was told that if I did not show up for the appearance, the cabbie's ticket would be automatically dismissed.

It seemed I had a choice to make: To go to court and forgo the obligation to my client or miss court and hope for the best. However, before I made the decision in favor of serving my client, I realized it was important for me to know if the driver of the taxi had struck other pedestrians. Was this his pattern of behavior? If yes, I felt a responsibility as a member of society to make sure he was penalized. This required research.

First, I asked some attorneys to see if there was a way to get the court date changed. I learned from them that what my staff had discovered was indeed true. The date was set and could not be changed.

Then I inquired if they could help me find out if this taxi driver had done this before to someone else. Each person referred me to someone else until I was able to learn that this taxi driver had a valid driver's license, had no outstanding warrants or tickets and had not done this before. So, I said a prayer of thanksgiving for my good health and well-being, and decided it was OK if I skipped the court date. My gift was my life, my health, my physical being and most of all my new outlook of happiness and joy.

So the appointed court date of October 5 came and went, just as I was traveling to and from my business meeting in another state. That day came and went without me giving it another thought. Life was moving on...or so I thought.

About a month later, I received a letter from the City of Chicago Department of Law. Upon opening it, I was stunned to see that I was being compelled to come to court on November 17. Specifically the form letter with the boxes filled in stated, "You are listed as a complaining witness or as an eyewitness in a case now pending in Traffic Court. The case was continued so that you could be notified in the event that you wish to testify. If you wish to testify, you should appear at: Richard J. Daley Center, 50 West Washington Street, Chicago, IL 60602 on November 17, 2014."

The ticket had not been automatically dismissed as I was told it would be. The judge was giving me the opportunity to appear in court as a witness to the accident. I remember thinking that witness was the wrong term. I was the victim. So I placed the date on my calendar while also realizing that something or someone was making this happen. In talking with my friends who have worked in traffic court and as assistant district attorneys (ADAs), I learned none of them had ever seen this happen.

So on the appointed date of November 17th, 2014 at 11 a.m., I arrived at the Richard Daley Center in the traffic court, with my mother in tow. She happened to be visiting me and was determined to see the man who had hit her daughter while driving his taxi. I asked my mom to sit in the back of the courtroom and went up to the front to sign in as required.

The ADA said, "You're Lisa Dietlin?"

"Yes."

"We thought you would be in a body cast."

"No..."

"So, you're OK?"

"Yes."

She asked me to follow her to the hallway so we could confer. Once outside the courtroom, she said, "The taxi driver is here and has an attorney with him."

I said nothing but thought, "F*%k! I should have brought my own attorney!"

"He wants to plead guilty but to a lesser charge."

"What charge?"

"Disobeying traffic patterns."

I responded saying, "Well…a friend who is personal injury attorney told me that having someone admit guilt is a good thing…I mean if I wanted to pursue a personal injury case."

"Of course. Most personal injury attorneys would be happy with this admission of guilt."

"Will he still be able to drive a taxi?"

"Yes."

"Good, because I don't want to 'jam' him up or ruin his livelihood."

So we went back into the courtroom and I sat next to my mom in one of the last rows. I was ready to wait; the courtroom was packed. But to my great surprise, the judge called my case first.

She asked for the taxi driver to come forward. He did, with his attorney standing beside him. The judge said something to them. She then asked for me to come forward. As I did, the taxi driver and attorney parted so I could walk between them to stand in front of the judge. What follows is my recollection of what was said and what happened.

"Lisa, the court is so glad to see you here. We were worried when you were not here last month."

"My apologies, your honor, I had a conflict and it seemed we couldn't get the court date changed."

"Are you all right?" she inquired.

I replied, "Yes, your honor. I'm fine."

"Are you OK with the decision for him to plead guilty to a lesser charge?"

"Yes, I am, but he will still get to drive a taxi, right? I mean I don't want him not to be able to make a living."

The judge responded assuring me he could still drive a taxi even by pleading guilty to this charge. Again, she iterated that she and the court were happy to see me doing so well.

I then stepped back as the judge called the defendant (taxi driver) and his attorney forward. She said he would be found guilty of violating traffic patterns, and he'd have to pay a fine. Then she banged the gavel down.

It was at that point something profound and again life changing happened.

The taxi driver turned towards me and lunged. Startled, I realized he was lunging to hug me. He was crying and his voice was muffled, but I heard him say, "I am so sorry. I didn't know what had happened to you. I am so sorry. I was so worried."

I hugged him back, still startled, saying, "I'm OK. It's OK."

He kept holding onto me and crying. Then he took a deep breath and let go.

I looked at him and said, "It's really OK." He lunged again, hugging me even tighter, still sobbing. I kept assuring him I was OK, and that it was all right.

At this point I caught the eye of the judge, who was smiling down on us from the bench. As the taxi driver and I parted the second time, I grabbed his hand and said, "We need to go to the back of the courtroom. We're holding up the court proceedings."

We then walked hand-in-hand to the back of the courtroom and one more time he turned to hug me for a third time, still sobbing, still apologizing. And again I said, "It's really OK. I'm fine." As we parted I squeezed his hand, looked him in the eye and said, "Go and have a good life."

And then I gave his hand one more squeeze and let go. That was the last time I saw him.

Truly this man had been tortured for two and a half months while wondering what had happened to the woman who took a ride on the hood of, and then got under the wheels of, his taxi. I can only imagine the pain, suffering and angst he felt prior to each court date, wondering if I would show up, what condition I was in and what I would do, as well as how his life would be further changed by all of it.

Had he seen my response as a gift? I know I had...but we each had our own perceptions.

For me, the gift was transformation. I was grateful for my life and truly forgave the driver for what happened to me. The combination of forgiveness and gratitude was the best medicine for a speedy recovery...just like *The New York Times Magazine* story of the card covered in sparkles featuring a bouquet of roses received in the mail by René Steinke from the bus driver was enough for her healing to begin.

And, truth be told, I know very little about the driver of the taxi except he was a man who cared and was affected by what had happened...and that was enough for me.

CHAPTER 6
Changes in Me

Change.
Change is good for you.
Change is difficult.
People can't change.
People can change.

All of these are statements many people have heard often. My guess is many of them believe all to be true. But, which ones are true? Is change possible? Can people change? What needs to happen for change to occur? In my case, big change occurred after being literally knocked off my feet. So, what changes occurred in my life after this accident and its legal resolution in court?

First, I'm an optimist who believes change can and does happen. My accident proved this to me. Initially, a couple of things changed in me. The first thing I realized is that I had no concept of time anymore. This means my worry that went along with being on time, getting somewhere on time and not being late went away. Before the accident I was always obsessed with not being late.

If I was stuck in traffic or if a meeting ran long, I was always worried about being late for whatever was next on my schedule. This meant I was immediately checking out of whatever I was doing or I would stop listening to that with which I was supposed to be paying attention all the while trying to figure out how to get back on time. Riding in a car with me was never fun especially if we were running late. My anxieties got the best of me and I'd be stressed first about being late and second about what steps needed to be taken to remedy the situation.

In other words, a lot of time was spent on asking questions in order to make a Plan B, and to make it fast:

"Is there an alternate way to get there?"

"Do we have a cell phone number of the contact?"

"Can we call in to the meeting?"

"Do we know where we are going to park?"

The questions were a way to keep my energy spinning! It was as if I could control the world just by demanding answers. Then there was my focus on when other people arrived for meetings and work. "Why doesn't anyone pay attention to these details?" was a question I kept asking myself. Don't get me wrong, I think there is an importance to arriving on time and being on time—after all, first impressions are still important. You certainly would not want to be late for an interview, critical meeting or an appointment if it had been made with me. Before the accident, I lived by William Shakespeare's quote, "Better three hours too soon than a minute late."

My obsession with time was a constant companion until the being hit and struck by a taxi.

After the accident, I noticed that time, which had slowed down during my ride on the hood of the taxi, continued to move in a slower manner. For example, the next day seemed to last forever. It was if I had all the time in the world. Everything I wanted to get done that day got done; even the love letter emails to my friends and important people in my life. As the days went by, I found time to talk with everyone on my list, accomplish various work projects and even take on some new challenges.

Even now, when I get stuck: in traffic, on a phone call or anything else that detracts me from my time schedule, I automatically shift my thinking to a better place. I assume everything is unfolding the way it is supposed and that there is a reason I am running late. Realizing I've forgotten something and returning home to get it? Now instead of cursing, I realize that the act might have saved me from another sort of 'hit' that could be far more unfortunate!

Lessons regarding time continued to unfold in amazing and perfectly timed ways. On the day after the accident, I received an invitation from a colleague via Facebook to attend Oprah's event, "The Life You Want Weekend," in Detroit, Michigan. As incredulous as it seems and just mere hours after being struck by a taxi thinking I was going to die, I knew I had to attend this event.

The condition of receiving two free tickets was that I had to be accompanied by someone I was mentoring. My niece Anna was the person I asked; I am her mentor. When I called to ask her, Anna said, "I would love to go but my mom said you got hit and run over by a taxi. Are you sure you can attend?"

I told her that I was sure I could go and would meet her in Detroit.

When I told people I was going to the event, many thought I was crazy to even consider attending. They shared their concerns about my fitness to make the trip. My response to them was always the same: "Just how long am I supposed to wait to start living my life again?"

I appreciated their concern, but really, what was the magical timeframe that would allow me to live my life? Could I start doing things again tomorrow? The next day? The day after my doctor said I was fine? In a week? A month? There didn't seem to be a time frame into which healing from my unusual trauma could fit! Time was the issue, but I was now viewing it as an asset and something to be grasped with both hands.

My niece and I did attend Oprah's "The Life You Want Weekend" and had life changing experiences. Each of us realized something different about ourselves. We recognized that everyone is able to achieve their goals if only they believe and have clarity about their dreams while maintaining a joyful attitude towards life, remaining happy within all circumstances.

The experience of that weekend gave me perspective on what I had been missing; it was if the missing piece had been filled in. It told me that I needed to read the signs. The event started on Friday night as Oprah addressed 40,000 people at the Auburn Hills Palace. She told the story of her life, sharing the importance of listening to the "whisper" you hear. The "whisper" could be your intuition, your gut instinct, a higher power or simply a voice. If you still don't listen to that whisper, Oprah said that it will get louder. And if you still don't listen, Oprah believes the whisper turns into what appears to be bricks being thrown at you. This will continue until you hit a proverbial brick wall.

At this point in the presentation, when Oprah uttered these words, my niece turned to me and said, "I think you hit the brick wall when the taxi ran over you." I nodded and smiled while recalling all the whispers I had ignored and bricks I had dodged or endured in order to get where I was supposed to be and of course on time.

Here's a little history of my life before the brick wall appeared. It involves a message about forward motion in another vehicle in my life—a Jeep. Eleven months before the taxi hit me, the engine on my Jeep blew up on a road near the shores of Lake Superior as I was traveling to a meeting. But I continued on, even though there were no rental car stores open on Sunday in the Upper Peninsula of Michigan. To attend the client meeting, I rented a U-Haul moving van and of course, arrived on time. I now view the engine failure as a brick being tossed at me, encouraging me to make a course correction in my life.

A few months later, I was driving back to the Upper Peninsula to deliver a final report to the same client. On a Sunday morning from my hometown in northern Michigan, I left in the middle of a blizzard against the caution of all my cousins who were at a wedding reception with me the night before. They had been following the weather reports, which were urging extreme caution as even the five-mile-long Mackinac Bridge was being closed at times during the storm.

But I was invincible, or so I thought.

After crossing the "Mighty Mac," as the Mackinac Bridge is known to Michiganders, I realized the front left tire on my Jeep was low so I stopped in a gas station in St. Ignace to fill it. The air hose was frozen and I had to defrost it first. It was 27 below zero that morning. It was only after I had tried twice to fill the front left tire and decided I should get some gasoline that I noticed the front right tire was peeling away from the rim. That was the real issue.

After several hours of trying to find someone to change the tire, a young man agreed and a few hours later I was traveling back to my hometown, knowing I would completely miss the meeting, as there was no way I could arrive on time. A brick was once again being thrown at me.

Two months later, I was traveling back to Michigan for a meeting in East Lansing, then on to more meetings in the Detroit area. Against advice again, I left in the early morning hours during a blizzard with snow so thick and heavy the green highway signs were not visible! During this trip, my Jeep ended up going into a ditch backwards after spinning out of control on the highway. When the Michigan State trooper arrived, he was shocked to find that I had threaded the needle between two signs without a scratch on the Jeep. I now know it was another brick being thrown at me to help me slow down.

A few weeks later, in early April, I was traveling to a gym to work out at 5:30 in the morning. Stopping at a red traffic light, I noticed a large, white diesel pick-up truck pull up behind me and felt the driver's anxiety at how slow I'd gone through the intersection. As soon as possible, the driver accelerated and pulled into the right hand lane to pass me. His truck hit black ice and spun counterclockwise into my lane and hit my Jeep. The force of that impact pushed my car into the center lane, sliding and spinning.

The outcome? I maneuvered the Jeep to the side of the road and dialed 911 prior to checking on the driver of the pick-up truck. He was stuck on a tree that had split the cab from the bed of the truck.

I was sure he was dead or seriously injured. He was OK, and told me that he'd been worried about me when he saw my car sliding and spinning. For two hours, we waited together in my Jeep for the police to arrive, chatting and becoming fast friends in that short amount of time.

In "Oprah language," this was another brick being thrown at me, telling me a course correction was necessary. I needed to start paying attention. But as usual I didn't. Again I was thinking I was invincible and that I had to continue working. To keep moving forward…or so I thought.

Then there was the taxi accident. I now view the accident as the brick wall I hit. I had to stop what I was doing and make a correction. Life was screaming at me to make changes to be happy and joyful. But would I listen? Would I be able to make that change?

The answers are yes. Now I listen to the whisper, to my gut, to my intuition. Daily I try to make sure I have clear perspective on what I want to do and don't want to do.

CHAPTER 7

What I've Learned

When you go through a traumatic experience as I did, you learn things about yourself.

You also learn things about the world. And if you are lucky, you are able to take those things and live a better and perhaps even more meaningful life. Here are a few things I learned.

Lesson #1
Life will always work out.

This is a statement I believe. Life does work out as it is supposed to, but your choices and attitude play a major part. American patriot and inventor Ben Franklin is credited with saying, "Do not squander time, it's the stuff life is made of," and he is right.

Use your time wisely. Focus on what is important. After all, no one on their deathbed ever said, "I wished I had spent more time at work." And being known as a hard worker is not something most of us would want as the lead in our obituary or on our headstone. Follow your intuition and gut. Listen to the whisper.

Lesson #2
Go for it!

What I learned is that there is only so much time each of us has on this Earth. It is important to go for whatever it is. You never know when your time will be up. It could be this afternoon or tomorrow morning, next week, next year or ten years into the future. But the day is coming. Do the things you have always wanted to do.

Create a bucket list. Check off the items as you accomplish those things you most want to do.

Before the accident I was always willing to try anything new with the caveat that it must fit nicely and neatly into my work schedule. Now I am committed to doing everything I can to expand my horizons and live a life filled with happiness and joy. Flying trapeze classes; a Tough Mudder competition; meeting new people; trying new foods; taking time for myself; reconnecting regularly with old friends without any hesitation; and taking chances are all things I greatly value today because of the accident. The Christmas following the accident, my good friend Erin gave me a book with the title, appropriately named for my new life, *Do One Thing Every Day That Scares You*. While I am not sure this is the best advice for everyone, it certainly is something to ponder when deciding if you should go for it.

Lesson #3
You can't take it with you.

When the accident happened, I was working on a personal fun project to watch all the Academy Award® Best Picture winners in chronological order. The next film that happened to be at my house waiting to be watched was the 1938 classic, "You Can't Take It with You," starring Jimmy Stewart and Lionel Barrymore. The message of the movie was that life is full of unexpected twists and turns but money can't buy you happiness or love. It's the people you love and experiences which in the end will matter the most.

Use what you have for the good because you can't take it with you. After watching this movie, I thought about how timely the message of this film was for me. All the things I might have put off until a better time, I needed to do. All the places I wanted to visit, or things I wanted to see and do, needed to be prioritized. Fun had to move up on the list of values as well as time spent with friends and family members.

Lesson #4
Do the things you love.

The next movie I received in the mail in this journey of watching the Academy Award® Best Pictures post the accident was the 1939 winner, "Gone with the Wind", a two-disc DVD package. I wondered when I'd have time to sit and watch four hours of a movie I had seen before and often caught in pieces when channel surfing.

Then I learned that the author of the book with the same title, Margaret Mitchell, had herself been struck and killed by an off-duty taxi cab driver. Mitchell died after lingering for five days in a hospital. Coincidence? Or a message from the Universe and God that I needed to make time to do the things I love to do which includes watching old movies? Now I make time to do things I love.

Lesson #5
Always wear good shoes and take care of yourself.

As you have surmised, I love shoes, especially my Donald J. Pliner shoes. It might sound silly but I believe that my Donald J. Pliner shoes were partially responsible for saving my life. They provided a sturdy platform on which I was able to walk and withstand being hit by a car traveling 35 mph.

I also was in good shape having had a lifelong commitment to working out daily for at least an hour.

And treat yourself to great underwear. You deserve it all the time, not just in case you end up in an emergency room!

Lesson #6
Life will throw you into unexpected situations; determine how you will respond.

Many people encouraged me to sue the cab driver and company after the accident. I viewed this as pointless because it would only focus on the negative aspect of the accident. Clearly, I was focused on the positive and I needed to follow the words heard in the hospital about the importance of happiness and joy.

Then I saw this short saying and thought that it sums up my new life perspective perfectly:

> One day she finally grasped that unexpected things were always going to happen in life and with that she realized the only control she had was how she chose to handle them. So she made the decision to survive using courage, humor and grace. She was the queen of her own life and the choice was hers.
>
> Queenisms™ on a weblog by Kathy Kinney at www.queenofyourownlife. com/blog/1358.

How will you respond to unexpected situations? This could include everything from a lost wallet or item to a personal betrayal, so focus on the emotions you feel when you're startled and think about the methods of self-soothing that work best for you. Then work to respond in that way. It might not always work but practice makes perfect.

Lesson #7
Memorize phone numbers, especially that of your ICE person.

With the advent of smart phones, we now make phone calls by simply typing in the name of a person or touching the name on screen of our phone. After the taxi incident, my phone went missing for a short time. The good Samaritans, James and Ryan, kept asking if they could call my ICE (In Case of Emergency) person. I did not know her phone number. Memorize the important numbers or have them written in an accessible place, and with you at all times.

Lesson #8
Always wear clean underwear.

Your mother was right. Enough said.

Lesson #9
Tell the ones you love that you love them.

Don't wait. There is no time like the present to share love with those who mean something to you. Do it today! My good friend, Jenniffer Weigel, often suggests writing and sending a love letter to someone each week. Try it. You will not only change their world, but yours, too.

Lesson #10
Remember, the great equalizer for all of us is time.

The author of this is unknown but the meaning is very memorable.

⏰ To realize the value of ONE YEAR, ask a student who failed a grade.

⏰ To realize the value of ONE MONTH, ask a mother who has given birth to a premature baby.

⏰ To realize the value of ONE WEEK, ask the editor of a weekly newspaper.

⏰ To realize the value of ONE HOUR, ask the lovers who are waiting to meet.

⏰ To realize the value of ONE MINUTE, ask a person who just missed a train.

⏰ To realize the value of ONE SECOND, ask someone who just avoided an accident.

⏰ To realize the value of ONE MILLISECOND, ask the person who won a silver medal at the Olympics.

Each of us is given 24 hours (1,440 minutes) every day and how we approach and react to those hours, as well as what we do with those hours determines a lot about life.

One of my graduate school classmates shared this on social media. It is from author Marc Levy's book, *If Only It Were True:*

Imagine there is a bank that credits your account each morning with $86,400. It carries over no balance from day to day.

Every evening at 11:59:59 p.m. the bank deletes whatever part of the balance you failed to use during the day.

What would you do?

Draw out every cent, of course?

Each of us has such a bank.

Its name is TIME.

Every morning, it credits you with 86,400 seconds.

Every night it writes off as lost, whatever of this you have failed to invest to a good purpose.

It carries over no balance. It allows no overdraft. Each day it opens a new account for you. Each night it burns the remains of the day.

If you fail to use the day's deposits, the loss is yours. There is no drawing against tomorrow.

You must live in the present on today's deposits.

Invest it so as to get from it the utmost in health, happiness and success!

The clock is running!! Make the most of today.

Treasure every moment that you have! And treasure it more because you shared it with someone special, special enough to spend your time with. And remember time waits for no one.

CHAPTER 8
Happiness and Joy Always

In this post-taxi cab accident world I'm living in,
I am always looking for signs, mottos and quotes to reinforce what the voice told me that night in the hospital about happiness and joy.

While attending a graduation breakfast given in honor of outstanding students in my hometown, one of the speakers distributed a card titled, "10 ½ Things No Commencement Speaker Has Ever Said" which was published in *The Wall Street Journal* and written by economist Charles Wheelan. One of the statements struck a chord with me as profoundly true: "Lead a life you will be happy with and proud of 10-20 years from now, that is if you don't get hit by a bus."

I thought it ironic to see this eight months to almost the date after my transformative experience on the hood of a taxi cab. Another reminder to focus on happiness and joy.

Remember that happiness is about circumstances; joy is about who you are. Both are essential, I believe, to the process of living a fulfilled life.

Here are some other things I believe ensure a happy and joyful life:

- Do something every day for yourself
- Do something every day for someone else
- See the good in everything and also try to see it in everyone
- Surround yourself with things that bring your happiness and joy

Additionally, these are my personal keys to daily happiness. Every day, I intend three things for myself—and I'm happy with even just one of them:

- To enjoy the experience of a good cup of coffee
- To exercise, and appreciate moving my body, for an hour each day
- To relax with a good glass of wine at the end of the day

These are small things, but each brings a smile to my face and provides a moment or two of happiness and joy each day. Determine three things that make you happy daily then work to ensure those things show up all together or even one-by-one in your life.

I also try to do these three things a day for other people and my community. My simple list is comprised of these things:

- Each day I pick up a piece of garbage and place it in the proper receptacle
- Each day I write and send a personal and heartfelt piece of correspondence to someone
- And finally, every day, I pay a genuine compliment to a person

In a world often filled with unfair comparisons and horrors like cyber-bullying, I saw these two items on social media. Both are so appropriate to living a life filled with happiness and joy.

The first one was found on LinkedIn with no attribution; it simply stated:

1. Don't let someone else's opinion of you become your reality.
2. Never let a bad day make you feel like you have a bad life.
3. It's never too late to be what you might have been.
4. If the opportunity doesn't knock, build a door.
5. Begin each day with a grateful heart.

And the second item which was found on Facebook is "Seven Keys to Greater Happiness" which encompasses the following (cited from the Advanced Life Skills website www.advancedlifeskills.com):

1. Free your heart from negative feeling.
2. Free your mind of pointless worries.
3. Choose simple over complex.
4. Avoid needless drama.
5. Stop judging others.
6. Love yourself.
7. Be grateful.

Do you allow yourself to be happy? Do you allow yourself to be joyful?

A quote I love by Persian poet Hafez is, "Fear is the cheapest room in the house. I would like to see you living in better conditions." A while ago I learned that **FEAR** is really an acronym for **F**alse **E**vidence **A**ppearing **R**eal. When I operate out of **FEAR**, it is never good and definitely full of assumptions and misconceptions none of which are ever true. Instead now, I choose to operate out of courage as well as happiness and joy.

To live a happy and joyful life, remove fear. Make changes in your life towards happiness and joy without having to suffer a traumatic event. Another way of considering this is to follow what I heard American inspirational speaker Iyanla Vanzant say: "Put yourself in a first class seat in your own life." Do you do this?

Recently, I came across a birthday card I had received before the accident. It shows a woman in a business suit walking barefoot on the edge of a shoreline carrying her shoes. The caption says, "Here's to knowing what matters most…and doing it!"

That's how I live my life now.

A life filled with happiness and joy!

How will you live yours?

A life of happiness and joy...some readers might think that it is something easy to achieve and others might think it is impossible. I am still on this journey sorting it out on a daily if not at times an hourly basis.

I do know that one does not need to be run over by a taxi, bus or bike to have a life changing experience. It is about where you focus your time, energy and attention.

For me, this final quote sums up how life should be approached and while not a Beatles music fan, I am happy to share what John Lennon is reported to have said about how life was explained to him at a young age.

> "When I was 5 years old, my mother always told me that happiness was the key to life. When I went to school, they asked me what I wanted to be when I grew up. I wrote down 'happy.' They told me I didn't understand the assignment, and I told them they didn't understand life."

Happiness and Joy always to all of you!

#happinessandjoy

Made in the USA
San Bernardino, CA
27 November 2016